GOD DOES NOT CREATE *Miracles*
YOU DO!

Distributed by Publishers Group West

GOD

DOES **NOT** CREATE

Miracles

YOU DO!

YEHUDA BERG

For further information:

The Kabbalah Centre
155 E. 48th St., New York, NY 10017
1062 S. Robertson Blvd., Los Angeles, CA 90035

1.800.Kabbalah www.kabbalah.com

First Edition March 2005
Second Printing July 2006
Printed in USA
ISBN 1-57189-306-7

Design: Hyun Min Lee

For the Rav . . .

TABLE OF CONTENTS

Table of Contents

ACKNOWLEDGMENTS

I would like to thank the many people who have made this book possible.

First and foremost, Rav and Karen Berg, my parents and teachers. I will be forever thankful for your continual guidance, wisdom, and unconditional support. I am just one of the many whom you have touched with your love and wisdom.

Michael Berg, my brother, for your constant support and friendship, and for your vision and strength. Your presence in my life inspires me to become the best that I can be.

My wife, Michal, for your love and commitment; for your silent power; for your beauty, clarity, and uncomplicated ways. You are the strong foundation that gives me the security to soar.

David, Moshe, Channa, and Yakov, the precious gifts in my life who remind me every day how much there is to be done to ensure that tomorrow will be better than today.

Billy Phillips, one of my closest friends, for your help in making this book possible. The contribution you make to The Kabbalah Centre every day and in so many ways is appreciated far more than you could possibly know.

To Andy Behrman, thank you for your consistent and passionate pursuit of truth and for committing your talents to helping our team make a difference in this world.

To Hyun Lee, Christian Witkin, and Esther Sibilia, whose contributions made the physical quality and integrity of everything we do live up to the spiritual heritage of this incredible wisdom that has been passed on to me by my father, Rav Berg.

I want to thank Rich Freese, Eric Kettunen, and all the team at PGW for their vision and support. Your proactive efficiency gives us the confidence to produce more and more books on Kabbalah so that the world can benefit from this amazing wisdom.

To all the Chevre at The Kabbalah Centres worldwide— the evenings we share together in study fuel my passion to bring the power of Kabbalah to the world. You are a part of me and my family no matter where you might be.

To the students who study Kabbalah all over the world —your desire to learn, to improve your lives, and to share with the world is an inspiration. The miracles I hear from you every day make everything I do worthwhile.

GOD NEVER DID IT!

God Does Not Create Miracles! A book title like this may sound like blasphemy—or at least like a profane allegation made by some radical atheist—but before you slam this book shut I assure you that that this is not the case. According to the ancient wisdom of Kabbalah, not only is it true that God does not create miracles, but the reasons for this allows for God to be even more kindly disposed to humankind than you might have supposed.

Look at it this way. If God is only good, if God is all-powerful, do you really believe He would perform miracles for one person and not for another if both people were equally in need? Do you really believe God plays favorites?

One person is miraculously healed from a disease whereas another person continues to suffer. Do you really accept, in your heart of hearts, the old standard response: *God works in mysterious ways?*

And if God *does* respond to a prayer and heals a sick person, why would He stop there? In other words, if someone is confined to a wheelchair and then miraculously gets up and walks because of God's willingness to perform a miracle, why doesn't God also throw in the miracle of immortality and endless happiness for this person as well? What kind of miracle is it if you're healed from one disease only to eventually wind up dying later from some other cause? This clearly implies a limitation in the power of a God-given miracle.

THE TOUGH QUESTIONS

If these questions have not yet given you reason to wonder about God's involvement in the making of miracles, here are few more:

If God performed all the miracles spoken of in The Bible, why wouldn't God perform the greatest miracle of all—ending all suffering, disease, sadness, and death in the world?

Are you to believe that God can part a Red Sea but He can't part the sea of chaos that overwhelms this world?

If He can, then why doesn't He?

If He can't, can you truly say God is all-powerful?

Now think about this:

If God is *only* good, if God is *infinite* in His power, miracles should happen all the time. They should occur every day. Every hour. Every moment that you need them. Why should a human being suffer for even five minutes if God can miraculously transform the whole world in a nanosecond?

What is God waiting for?

Only one thing:

He's waiting for you!

THE TRUE PRODUCER OF MIRACLES

If you don't have the courage to ask the tough questions, you'll never understand the ancient formula for true miracle making. On the other hand, if you *are* ready to ask those tough questions, profound answers and miracles await you in the pages that follow.

Let's begin by understanding God's role in our lives, in this world, and in the appearance of a bona fide miracle.

Understanding God

Kabbalah says God is all-powerful. Kabbalah says God is only good. In fact, no chaos, suffering, negativity, or tragedy of any kind can be attributed to God.

For instance, consider the meaning of the word *good*. *Good* means *only* good. Period. It doesn't include anything negative or bad. Thus, bad can't emerge from good. It's illogical.

God is defined as the *greatest* possible good. Therefore, no bad can ever emerge from God. And that means *ever*.

That being said, God still does *not* perform miracles for you. It is *you* who cause miracles to take place, knowingly or unknowingly. It is also *you* who answers your own prayers.

Please don't panic. This does not, in any way, diminish God's role as the *true source* of all miracles and goodness in the world. So, you see, this book is not really blasphemous at all.

I know what you're asking yourself:

> *How, then, do we reconcile the notion that God does not perform miracles but God still remains the ultimate source of all miracles?*

Finally, after a few thousand years, someone is asking the right question!

God's Role in Miracle Making

According to Kabbalah, God is an infinitely powerful and positive force. *You* create your own miracles when *you* successfully *connect* to this infinite force of goodness—*connection* being the key concept here.

However, it is your effort; your work; your physical, emotional, and spiritual exertion that brings about the miracles in your physical world. You see, for reasons that will be explained shortly, it takes great effort to truly connect to God.

THE POWER OF CONNECTION

Here is a simple but deeply profound analogy that will finally resolve thousands of years of misunderstandings concerning God, human suffering, unanswered prayers, and the all-too-rare occurrences of miracles in the world.

Imagine a massive, darkened auditorium. It's pitch black. Inside the auditorium stand three people. They're uncomfortable, stranded alone in the darkness. So the first person prays to the electricity to power up the lights. Nothing happens. The second person hastily erects a tiny synagogue, church, or mosque inside the auditorium to worship the electricity in the hopes that it will activate the lights. Still nothing happens. The first two people then get together and write on parchment scrolls in praise of this unseen force and speak of it in story and parable. Nothing happens.

The third person sits for a while and then patiently moves over to the light switch and flips it on. The auditorium is instantly bathed in light.

In this overly simple example, the electricity is analogous to the Light of the Creator. The force of electricity never consciously refuses a request to power up your home appliances or lamps. Nor does the force of God refuse to answer your prayers for miracles. In fact, an all—merciful and all—compassionate God, by definition, would never say "No!" to a request. If you want to talk about something being blasphemous, I personally believe it would be blasphemous to believe—even for a second—that God could possibly refuse a prayer or even that He works in mysterious ways.

So, what's the underlying problem? Why all the turmoil in your midst? Why do your prayers go unanswered?

Just as a lamp must first be plugged into electrical current to receive its power, you too must *plug in* to the force of God to receive the power of miracles.

Electricity is *always* there. It is always present, ready, able, and willing to fulfill all of your power needs—*if you just plug in!* The force of God works the exact same way. This force is everywhere and in everything, but you must know *how* it works and then take active steps to make the connection.

My father once told me that having the right phone number is not enough. You have to pick up the phone and dial if you want to connect to the other party and get a response.

From now on, consider the wisdom in this book to be God's phone number. Practicing this wisdom is how you dial—*toll-free.*

THE REASON FOR THE DARKNESS

To help you begin to understand why suffering occurs in the world, the electricity analogy works strikingly well. If you plug a toaster into a wall socket to make toast, you prepare the food that gives you life. If you stick your finger in a wall socket, all you get is an electric shock, along with some nasty pain, possibly accompanied by a short circuit that cuts the power to your house so you wind up in darkness.

The problem with the world is this: For the last few thousand years, humankind has been living with its finger in the wall socket. The result has been a world of darkness and a whole lot of hurt.

Now there is hope. Not only will this book teach you how to create miracles through a safe connection to the infinite force we call God, but it will also help you pull your own finger out of that socket so you finally put an end to all the short circuits in your own life.

THE NEED FOR EFFORT

Many religions tell you that the presence of God is everywhere and that all you have to do is appreciate and be aware of this presence in order to draw it into your life.

Kabbalah says, *If only it were that simple*. Many people appreciate the presence of God and still they do not achieve the miracles they need. Granted, they might achieve some comfort during a personal crisis or tragedy by thinking that the presence of God is near, or believing that God has a reason for their misfortune. This approach might help them cope more effectively.

However, this is where Kabbalah draws the line.

Kabbalah is not about coping or finding comfort during times of chaos. Kabbalah is about *curing* chaos and *correcting* the root cause of crises so they vanish without a trace.

From Cope to Cure

Life was never meant to be about coping with problems or finding comfort during a catastrophe. It's about curing whatever ails you and creating a world of unending happiness. Settling for anything less is to deny the truth of God's infinite goodness and His desire to share His Light with the world.

Appreciation, awareness, and faith just aren't enough. If you were stranded in a dark room, appreciating and recognizing the existence of electricity would not turn on the lights. You must take physical action—such as walking over to the on-off switch and flipping it to the on position.

If Not Now, When?

Making miracles is about effort, not faith. It's about doing a bit of work, not investing a lot of belief or acknowledgement in an unseen force. It's about taking action *now*, as opposed to waiting for some supernatural force to intervene on your behalf at some point in the future.

There's an actual formula, a practical technique for making this connection and achieving the miracles you need. This is what Kabbalah is all about. This is what Kabbalah has always been about.

It answers your questions and provides you with tools. The world just didn't know it was available until very recently, which is why humanity's most challenging questions and deepest desires have remained unfulfilled.

But not any longer.

THE OLDEST QUESTIONS IN THE WORLD

We all come into the world asking the same big questions: What's the point of being alive? Why are our lives filled with so much pain and suffering? Is there really a Creator? Why do our prayers go unanswered? And how can we get past the pain to bring real joy and fulfillment into our lives?

You may have heard that mere mortals can't possibly answer such questions. Maybe you were told that only God knows the answers and you have to wait for the End of Days or the appearance of a Messiah to find out what's really going on.

The insights gleaned from Kabbalah provide those answers *right now*. And the *Promised Land* is the land you're living in at this very moment. Specifically, this wisdom and your proper use of it will make miracles a reality now and forever.

Where the Power Belongs

Kabbalah has always promised this power. Perhaps that's why the religious establishment despised and feared this ancient wisdom. It took the power of God out of the hands of organized religion and put it squarely where it belongs—*into the hands of the people.*

Making miracles happen has everything to do with you, and with harnessing your ability to control matter with your mind.

Control matter with my mind?

Yes. Absolutely. I know this might be a radical shift in your consciousness, but Kabbalah is all about realizing your true power.

Until now, you've probably thought of miracles as something outside your control. Or maybe you just haven't believed in miracles at all. When they've happened, you've dismissed them as sheer coincidence. You've believed that miracles may have happened in biblical days, but they're not part of our lives anymore.

Miracles aren't just a thing of the ancient past at all—and they don't just happen to "special" people. You don't need to be a holy and righteous individual or a great sage or an expert in Kabbalah to create miracles. Furthermore, religion, race, and gender have no impact whatsoever on miracle making. Everyone can make miracles happen, but most people simply don't know that they can or how.

So, are you ready to learn what Kabbalah has to teach you? Are you ready to bring miracles into your life?

Let's make it happen!

THE NEED FOR SKEPTICISM

If you're a skeptic, that's a good thing. The ancient kabbalists appreciated the value of skeptics a lot because skeptics are doing what they should be doing: thinking critically and questioning everything. I do the same thing, and I don't expect any less of you.

One of the cardinal rules of Kabbalah is that it's important to not just believe what you read, but to test out the truth for yourself.

You see, that very same skepticism you bring to the concept of miracles can help you see through the limitations of your physical existence. In fact, the first thing you should be skeptical about is the reality and authenticity of the world around you. Start questioning the reality of the chaos and problems all around you. Because according to science, the world in front of your eyes is nothing but an illusion!

Let's now pierce this illusion and discover the true nature of reality.

UNDERSTANDING REALITY

You're having a hard time right now. That's why you've picked up this book. Life feels like a struggle. Even on your best days, there's some form of chaos waiting for you around the corner. You might be suffering from depression. Stress. Maybe you're reeling from a breakup or a divorce. Like most people, you're also probably dissatisfied with your job, worried about being a good parent, or just exhausted from trying to pay off your debt.

You might have older parents who need your attention and care. You wish you had more support, time, money, and opportunities to do the things you really want to do with your life.

You're looking for a miracle. Or two. Or three. But your rational mind says, *Real miracles are just too good to be true. Happiness can't happen to me.*

All this grief, sadness, and hopelessness, according to Kabbalah, represents only 1% of true reality. We will call it the **1% Realm**.

The remaining 99% of reality is hidden behind a curtain. We will call this hidden reality the **99% Realm**.

The purpose of Kabbalah (and this book) is to help you see through the curtain that keeps you in the dark. This book is meant to open your eyes to the rest of your beautiful reality: the 99% of existence that you do not perceive with your five senses. That hidden 99% has so much more to offer you than the frustration, turmoil, and seeming unpredictability of your life. It holds the power of all your miracles.

Just imagine if you could connect into the 99% Realm whenever you felt like it!

Imagine! Every time you experienced that elusive sixth sense, you made contact with the 99%.

When one of your dreams came true, you were online with the 99%.

When a mistake turned out to be a blessing, when you happened to meet the right person at the right time, when the chips fell your way, somehow you were dialed into the 99%.

Basically, creative inspiration, million-dollar ideas, passion and enthusiasm for life, confidence, love, and feelings of security are all examples of accessing the 99%. In fact, according to Kabbalah, every positive discovery in history, every good invention, all the positive developments and progress made throughout the ages, took place when individuals plugged themselves into that powerful hidden realm.

Kabbalah and miracle making are about knowing how to access the 99% Realm whenever you need to.

THE 1% AND 99% REALMS

To help you better understand the nature of reality, let's return to our electricity analogy. The power of the electrical force is everywhere. It's in the walls of your home. It's in the skies. It's even in your own body. Dr. Rodolfo Llinas, a neuroscientist at New York University's School of Medicine, states:

> *"Our thoughts, our ability to move, see, dream, all of that is fundamentally driven and organized by electrical pulses."*

However, the force of electricity remains hidden from your senses until a streak of lightning reveals it to your eyes. Or when sparks fly as metal scrapes against the pavement. The electrical force is in a state of potential until a chandelier is switched on, revealing the light of a bulb. It remains inactive until a portable heater is plugged into it and your body feels the warmth.

For thousands of years, the world lived in darkness, without all the marvelous benefits that electrical power offers but which you now take for granted. In case you never stopped to think about it, take a moment; without electricity, there are no

> *TVs to entertain you; air conditioners to cool you; furnaces to warm you; computers to assist you; shopping malls in which to shop; high-rise office towers in which to work; elevators and escalators to take you up and down; blow dryers to dry you; movie theaters to thrill you; ovens, toasters, blenders, cake mixers, and fridges to help feed you; streetlamps and indoor lights to illuminate your way.*

And the list goes on and on.

All of these benefits and luxuries were hidden behind a curtain for thousands of years until the force of electricity was finally revealed and harnessed only a few decades ago.

This unseen force of electrical power is a metaphor for the 99% Realm.

All the happiness, joy, healing, fulfillment, and serenity you seek from life is hidden in the 99% Realm. The power of miracles is really all around you. You sense it. You can practically taste it. You know in your gut that it's everywhere, which is why you seek it out 24 hours a day. You innately know that happiness is right there at your fingertips, which is why life becomes so depressing and so darn frustrating when you lack it.

THE REALITY OF THE ILLUSION

There is something else you already know on a subconscious, soul level: Happiness is the only thing that is truly real. The darkness, the pain, and all those nasty problems are merely a mirage, an illusion, no different than the temporary darkness that's created when a light switch is in the off position. Flip the switch and the darkness vanishes. *Wow. What a miracle!*

Even the great scientist Albert Einstein believed that the world you perceive is really a phantasm, a construct of the five senses. As he put it,

> *"Reality is merely an illusion, albeit a very persistent one."*

So, yes, your problems are an illusion, and the sorry condition of this world is also an illusion—albeit a very convincing one! You can break this illusion when you connect to the hidden force that dwells in the 99% Realm. That's when the darkness in your life vanishes.

You call it a miracle because it disappears in an instant, but the fact is, it's the exact same principle as the darkened room analogy.

Why Skepticism Is So Natural

This book makes it all sound so simple. We talk about lightbulbs, electricity, and dark rooms, making the possibility of miracles seem all too easy. It is more difficult than that, but it's also very possible. Yet some of us remain doubtful. Some even bitterly scorn the whole idea of God, miracles, and prayers.

Don't judge such people too harshly, because skepticism is a necessary and natural part of this 1% *Realm. Why? Because* all of these remarkable truths concerning the wonders of God must be hidden from the rational mind. They are even hidden from all religions and philosophies. After all, religion tends to divide people and bring about bloodshed. Bloodshed and God don't go together, so divine truths can't be found within organized religion. William Shakespeare, besides being one of the most prolific playwrights in history, was also a student of Kabbalah. In fact, to this very day, Shakespeare's Globe Theater still has massive kabbalistic images painted on the ceiling. Anyway, Shakespeare said it best in the words spoken by Hamlet:

> *"There are more things in heaven and earth, Horatio, than are dreamt of in your philosophy."*

In other words, you can only find truth when you question this 1% world of illusion and peek into the 99% Realm.

Now that you understand the true nature of reality according to Kabbalah, let's examine the true nature of human beings.

UNDERSTANDING HUMAN NATURE

Like Mother Nature, human nature has two aspects:

- **The 1% You**
- **The 99% You**

The 1% You is your rational mind, your ego. The 1% You, only believes what it can see. It is a cynic. It is full of fear. It is your reactive impulses. It is your reflex emotions. And it includes all of your instinctive, automatic behavioral responses to every event it witnesses and to everything it experiences. It is the ultimate automatic pilot.

The 1% You has no self-control—*at all!* The entire external world is like one giant trigger that constantly sets off a reaction within the 1% You. Your reaction might be anger. Jealousy. Anxiety. Fear. Vengeance. Envy. Conceit. Worry. Panic. Your reactions *also* might include happiness. Joy. High self-esteem.

In other words, if someone hurts you—physically or emotionally—the 1% You reacts to the pain. And if someone pays you a compliment, the 1% You reacts to the praise. In *both* cases, the 1% You has no control over its feelings. It merely *reacts*. Something *external* controls it. Something outside yourself elicits a response within you. That, my friend, is behaving like a robot.

Fortunately, you have another aspect. The 99% You is the *authentic you*. It is your soul. It knows all the truths of life. It is always proactive, never reactive. Just as electricity is invisible, locked in a state of potential, the 99% You also remains undetectable to your rational mind. In fact, the soul part of you is so well hidden, you don't even believe it exists. For thousands of years, billions of people who lived on this earth never even imagined the existence of electrical power. Nevertheless, it was always there. And so it is with your soul and the 99% Realm.

HOW TO CONNECT TO AND UNLEASH THE 99% YOU

Stop reacting—*to everything*. Period.

I didn't say hold in your feelings. I didn't say suppress all your reactions and responses. I said stop reacting. Period. Let it go. Everything. Completely.

What Happens When You Stop Reacting

The moment you stop reacting like a robot, your consciousness shifts to the 99% You. Your soul is unleashed. Which is a good thing for the following reasons:

Comparing Mother Nature and Human Nature

Both you and the world around you are structured according to the same 1% and 99% ratio.

- The 1% Realm consists of evil, darkness, and chaos. The 1% You consists of selfish impulses, dark desires, and the forces of chaos such as the aging of the body.

- The 99% You consists only of Light, goodness, and miracles—such as the miracle of life and the complexity of a healthy human body.

- Chaos happens in the world when we, as a people, disconnect from the 99% Realm. Darkness happens in your personal life when you disconnect from the 99% You.

When people allow themselves to be governed and dominated by their 1% Self, reacting to everything around them, responding to urges and impulses that fire every moment of the day, then the entire world is governed by the 1% Realm of chaos and turmoil.

Why?

Because the world is merely a reflection, a mirror of the individual self. The world of self and the world *out there* are intimately intertwined. For that reason, the collective behavior of humankind determines the condition of the world.

Right about now, the ego usually pipes in and says, "I find that hard to believe." If you want to hang onto your chaos, simply agree with the ego and close this book now. But if you want to test-drive Kabbalah to see if it really works, tell your ego to quiet down, and then turn the page.

HOW TO BECOME AN ISLAND IN A SEA OF CHAOS

If the majority of the world lives under the influence of the 1% Self, meaning people allow their egos to react to everything, then the world will mirror this behavior. Problems will plague the planet—economically, politically, socially, and environmentally.

Just look around.

If, however, you as an individual decide to stop reacting to all the selfish impulses coming from your 1% Self, you'll immediately make contact with the 99% You. In turn, you'll make contact with the 99% Realm. Goodness and Light will now shine upon you, though all around there may be darkness and despair. This is called a miracle.

By now you should be asking yourself (and this book) three challenging questions:

*1. Why is the world divided into two—the 1%
Realm and the 99% Realm?*

*2. Why do I consist of two aspects—the 1%
Me and the 99% Me?*

*3. Whose bright idea was it to create the world
and humans according to this 99-to-1 ratio?*

As we discussed earlier, Kabbalah is all about asking the tough questions and demanding real answers. So, are you demanding? Good. You'll receive your answers the minute you grasp the actual reason for the existence of the world. Yep—that's the big question that has hung over the world for thousands and thousands of years. (In a nutshell, why are we here?) Who would have believed that the answer to the most haunting question of all time would be found in this simple little book?

Let's find out what that answer is.

WHY OUR WORLD (AND YOU) EXIST

The world exists for one reason and one reason only: so you can have a place of your own where you can develop the skill of miracle making. Why would you need a place of your own and why would you want to develop such a talent?

When God created the souls of humanity, the act of creation was a miracle in and of itself. God then gave His miraculous creation all the joy and happiness anyone could possibly imagine. Wow! Another miracle. But like a child who has practically everything, we humans wanted just one more thing—the ability to be miracle makers just like our Creator.

Why?

Who's Your Daddy?

You're 17 years old. You've reached an age where you could really use your own form of transportation. So your dad buys you a set of wheels—a 27-speed bicycle to get you from *A* to *B*.

Although you appreciate the fact that you have your own mode of transportation, it would be even better if you had access to Dad's car—a brand-new Jaguar—whenever you went out with your friends.

So you ask your daddy, and he agrees. Except, instead of handing you the car keys, Dad drives you and your friends everywhere you want to go. Okay, it's not the ideal situation but it's better than sitting at home. What you really want, however, are Dad's keys so you can use the Jag whenever you like.

In other words, it's one thing being driven around by your dad, even though you're in a nice car. However, it's way better when you can drive the vehicle on your own. Granted, this is not a sophisticated analogy, but the principle at work is quite profound. God originally gave us *all* the happiness in the world. But only God held the keys to miracle making, which included the miracle of *creating all the happiness that God bestowed upon us.*

We had everything in the world but that. It's one thing being handed all the happiness in the world for free. It's far more fulfilling when we can conjure up all that happiness through the power of *our own* miracle making. God could do that. We couldn't. So we asked for that gift as well.

The Puzzle of Human Existence

Imagine a parent giving her child the coolest SpongeBob SquarePants jigsaw puzzle *already* assembled. Sure, it's nice to have the toy, but it would be lots more fun for the kid to have it *disassembled* at first, so he could put it together through his own effort.

Creating the miracle of unending happiness was the greatest happiness of all. So we asked for the chance to create it.

And because God's original intent was to give us *everything*, He could not say no when we asked for the power to create our own miracles, just like God does Himself.

So God agreed.

But there was a problem. And to understand the severity of this problem, let's first change the words *miracle making to Light making* and use a simple analogy to explain why we are on this dark and dangerous planet.

THE LIGHT-MAKING METAPHOR

Suppose you wanted to experience what it feels like to create simple illumination. You are given a box of candles and you're placed on a sun-soaked field in the middle of the day. Can you really appreciate the ability to create light with just your tiny candles? Not at all. The blazing sun shines 400 trillion watts of sunlight onto the earth every second. Compare that to a tiny flickering candle flame. The candlelight is insignificant in such a setting.

THE PURPOSE OF THIS PLANET

When the souls of humanity were first created, we were all unified as one single great soul. In other words, just as one shining ray of white sunlight contains all the individual colors of the rainbow, this one great shining soul contained all the individual souls that would ever be.

This one unified soul, which included you and me, existed in a realm where miracles were the norm and disorder and pain were nonexistent. As a result, we could never truly experience the fulfillment associated with creating our own miracles. We could not practice creating order out of chaos because chaos didn't exist.

So we entered a temporary reality—this earth—where the power of miracles and endless happiness was hidden. One soul shattered into individual pieces, creating the illusion of fragmentation, of me and you. This gave us an opportunity in which we could learn the art of miracle making through our interactions with one

GOD DOES NOT CREATE *Miracles* YOU DO!   55

another. It is a realm where miracles are so scarce, we don't believe in them. It is a world where darkness and chaos are the norm and therefore darkness and chaos are the only things that feel real, tangible, and believable to us. It is a realm where the true Creator has been hidden and thus the reality of God has remained totally alien to us. This realm fosters a "me" mentality, because we are now blinded to the underlying unity that binds all people as one.

Do you know why these truths concerning our existence have been unknown for millennia? Because they've been hidden behind the curtain, waiting for us to discover them.

Do you know why most people are cynical about the possibility of miracle making? Because the truths concerning miracles have been hidden behind that same curtain.

Do you know why there is so much conflict and intolerance between people, nations, and religions? Because the truths of our shared origin and unity are also there behind that curtain.

That curtain includes your very own ego.

For that reason, when you try to grasp these universal truths with your 1% Self, you *can't* do it. Not in a real, genuine, life-transforming way. The best you can do is grasp them intellectually, and even then, these truths do not motivate and inspire you to dramatically change who you are. You don't curse your own foot if you suddenly trip over it, because it's part of your own body. Yet you still curse your friends and foes when they hurt you, because you don't feel the truth—that they're part of your own spiritual body.

It doesn't have to stay that way. It was never meant to stay that way. In fact, the opportunity to change everything was handed over to us a few thousand years ago.

EMPOWERING THE HUMAN RACE

Kabbalah was originally given to humankind many long centuries ago as a tool for personal transformation so that we could grow, evolve, and develop the skills needed for genuine miracle making. (Just *how* we do that will be discussed shortly. You've waited thousands of years to finally learn this ancient art, so a few more moments won't make much difference.)

What really took place with Moses on Mount Sinai some 3,400 years ago was that Moses received the technology of Kabbalah in order to connect this world to the 99% Realm.

Multiple Dimensions

According to Kabbalah, the 99% Realm actually consists of nine hidden dimensions that you can't perceive. When you add these nine to our physical dimension, you get ten dimensions in total. Moses was able to plug our world into the other nine dimensions (the 99% Reality), allowing Light and miracles to flow into our world.

An Ancient Code

You see, the whole biblical story of Moses ascending to the top of Mount Sinai is really an encoded message. It's about Moses ascending into higher spiritual dimensions, or the 99% Realm.

Chances are, you heard that Moses came down from the mountain with the Ten Commandments inscribed on two tablets. Now brace yourself for the oldest and most provocative secret of Kabbalah.

There are no Ten Commandments.

The two tablets are a code, representing the two realms (the 1% and 99%). The term Ten Commandments is code for the ten dimensions. The story of the Ten Commandments tells us that the two realms were connected to each other, and the power of miracles and Light flowed through all ten dimensions, bringing our world into a state of paradise. That's what Mount Sinai was all about.

How's that for code cracking?

MIRACLES OF THE BIBLICAL KIND

It was Kabbalah that Moses used to connect our world to the 99% Realm. It was Kabbalah that Moses used to part the waters of the Red Sea. It was Kabbalah that Moses used to perform the miracle of the ten plagues that struck Egypt. And it was Kabbalah that Moses used to draw water from a rock when the Israelites griped about being hot and thirsty in the desert.

Contrary to popular belief, contrary to what all the rabbis, priests, ministers, bishops, televangelists, and Sunday school teachers have been telling you, God did *not* create those miracles.

Moses did!

And he used the technology of Kabbalah.

MIRACLES OF THE JESUS KIND

By the way, Jesus (originally known as Joshua, the son of Joseph) was also a master of Kabbalah. It was Kabbalah that Jesus used to perform all his miracles, including the miracle of healing. That's why he was known as the Son of God. In fact, the term *Son of God* originates and first appears in the most important book of Kabbalah, *The Zohar*. But just as Kabbalah was purposely kept from the masses by the religious establishment, so too was this ancient historical fact.

So, what does *Son of God* really mean?

Son of God, according to *The Zohar*, refers to *everyone* and *anyone* who masters the art of miracle making through the technology of Kabbalah. *The Zohar* calls such a person "the Son of God; the Son of the Holy One; the son of the Father." Furthermore, *The Zohar* says that when a person attains this level of miracle making, "There is no separation between the son and the Father. They are one. And all the treasures of the

Father's house are there for the son to use."

In other words, Kabbalah gives you the keys to Daddy's Jag anytime you choose.

This ancient secret is so explosive that most modern-day translations of *The Zohar* mysteriously omit these riveting verses.

WHAT WENT WRONG

So, what happened? Why didn't the people of Moses'generation or the generation of Jesus acquire the skill of miracle making and change our world forever? The ability to transform this existence into heaven on earth was right at their fingertips!

Why did they fail?

One reason: The people would not let go of their 1% Self. They refused to give up their egos.

Don't judge them harshly for blowing that once-in-a-lifetime opportunity. *You* do it every day. Every hour. Every minute. You choose your ego over your soul all day long.

Each time you react with impatience, anger, worry, envy, intolerance, judgment, fear, panic, jealousy, and every other emotion connected to the 1% You, you make the same decision as did the people of

Moses'time. You choose your ego over the power to perform miracles.

Is it any wonder that the world has suffered, generation after generation, since ancient times?

Not only did we allow our robotic and reactive 1% consciousness to control our lives, we never even knew that this egocentric consciousness existed as a separate part of ourselves.

We had no idea that our true selves and our true longings and desires were hidden behind the constant barrage of urges, reflexes, whims, and selfish impulses that rule the airwaves of our minds.

Now we do.

BREAKING AWAY

The technology of Kabbalah that was given to Moses provides you and me with the power to break free of our egos, to break free of our 1% Selves, and to connect to the 99% Realm where miracles are a dime a dozen.

Once you eradicate your ego *completely*—which takes a lifetime or two—you will have the power to heal yourself at will and to transform your pain into pleasure. You will acquire absolute control over the physical world and joy will be yours for the taking. If you don't believe that this is your ultimate destiny, you've just bought into the illusion of the 1% Realm and the 1% You!

Make no mistake: Your ego is strong. It doesn't want you to let go. It doesn't want to disappear, fading away into oblivion. That's okay. You're supposed to be doubtful, suspicious, and egocentric at first, just as you must first experience darkness in order to appreciate and understand the power of light.

But I think you'll agree: Thousands of years of cynicism, ego, and chaos are probably enough. Perhaps it's time to expose the illusion of this physical ego-based world for the hoax that it is, and to unleash the power of miracles and the power of the 99% You!

If you think it's time, if you're finally ready to let go of the chaos you've been supporting for many lifetimes, just turn the page and discover some long-hidden secrets concerning the ancient science of miracle making.

THE ANCIENT SECRET OF MIRACLE MAKING

Many decades ago, a great Kabbalist, Rav Brandwein, wrote a powerful letter to my father, Kabbalist Rav Berg. It was about understanding the nature of the universe and the formula for creating miracles. I have my father's permission to share some words from this letter with you.

The letter concerns the famous incident in The Bible known as the Parting parting of the Red Sea. For those not familiar with the story, here's a brief recap.

The Israelites, after being enslaved in Egypt for 400 years, are trying to escape to freedom. With the Egyptian army in hot pursuit, the Israelites are suddenly confronted by the Red Sea. They're trapped, and the army is rapidly closing in. Moses and the Israelites cry out to God to save them. God responds by asking Moses why he is wasting his time calling out to God.

Hmmmm. Obviously, that's not the kind of response you or I or Moses would expect or want from a compassionate God—a God who has the power to save us in the blink of an eye.

Even more strange, *God then tells Moses to send the Israelites into the sea.* That sounds more like a suicide mission than a miraculous act of salvation. But my father's teacher explains that this peculiar Bible story has encoded in it a powerful secret for creating miracles. The secret lies at the heart of this book and the technology of miracle making. So, read this book slowly and carefully, and maybe even two or three times.

Here's the excerpt from Rav Brandwein's letter:

> *After greeting you I wrote you a letter in response to your letter.*
>
> *"And God said to Moses, 'Why do you cry to me? Speak to the children of Israel, and tell them to march forward into the sea.'"*

Many have wondered about this. First, the words "to me" seem redundant. Who else could Moses have cried and prayed to if not to God? Second, the question "Why do you cry?" is also strange, as what could the children of Israel do in the midst of their trouble but cry and pray to their Father in heaven?

The answers are found in the teachings of The Zohar. God had already taught Moses everything he needed to know in order to control this perilous situation. For example, just as there are the natural laws of the physical world, there are natural laws in the spiritual world.

But sometimes one needs to attract a miracle which is outside nature, above all the natural laws. The only way one attracts a miracle is to rearrange the natural order that God has set up. This is achieved through an act of self-sacrifice.

In every man, the force of ego is innate and it motivates man to swallow up and rule over everything for the sake of his own existence. If he overcomes this ego, if he sacrifices his ego for the sake of connecting to the Light of the Creator, then this effort becomes a force that rises and tears away all the veils and obstacles. No power in the heavens is able to stop him or prevent him from receiving anything he asks for. His prayer will be answered in full.

Other great kabbalists explain this secret further through the verse "God is your shade." Just as the shadow imitates every movement of a man, so God does with man. If a man is willing to sacrifice his ego and rise above his inborn nature, God mirrors this effort and annuls all the natural laws of the world. And even if in the past a man was dishonest and is not deserving of a miracle, his genuine self-sacrifice and internal change of character will bring him salvation.

When God told Moses to tell the children of Israel to walk into the sea, this was an action that went directly against their inborn character. They were willing to risk death for the sake of the Creator. They were willing to demonstrate great conviction and certainty in the teachings God gave to Moses, even though their natural instinct was to be doubtful and fearful.

Their self-sacrifice altered the natural laws and made the sea into a dry land.

I have revealed a little yet a thousand times as much is concealed.

I hope to continue discussing this matter with you, for there are things that are not yet allowed to be written down. God willing, I will tell them to you when we will be together soon. Please let me know if you understand what I have written.

Wishing you all the best,
Yehuda Brandwein

So there it is. You now have the secret for conjuring up miracles. When you act according to your nature, the world around you will act according to the laws of nature. When you break from your inborn nature and transcend your ego, you transcend the natural laws of this world, including the laws of physics and the karmic laws of cause and effect.

THE MIRROR

Imagine that there was a ten-mile-wide mirror up above you in the sky. If you look up at the sky and cuss and deliver obscene gestures, what will the image in the mirror do? Exactly!

If you resist your desire to curse and, instead, you blow kisses to the sky, what does the great image in the mirror do in return?

When The Bible says that *man was created in the image of God*, this is one of the secrets it was trying to reveal. God and the universe will shower you with kindness and kisses when you demonstrate a little tolerance and kindness toward the nasty people in your life, resisting your hatred, jealousy, and all your justified anger. Yes, even if anger is justified, you lose. Because the mirror will simply reflect back your negative actions into this world, one way or another.

The 99% Realm reflects back your every action and move. When you create a miracle of behavior within yourself, the cosmos produces a miracle in return. So, why do you not always see results right away? One reason: *Time*. Time delays the payback. This delay gives you an opportunity to exercise free will. If you say, "Hey, it didn't work!" you've blown it. You've reacted. You've responded robotically to the time delay. If you resist doubt and demonstrate total certainty, knowing that your action will produce an effect at some point in the future, you've just behaved like a human being. And this, by the way, will speed up the arrival of the miracle.

So, let's examine the types of miracles that await you in the 99% Realm.

FOUR TYPES OF MIRACLES

There are four different types of miracles that you can create. These are important to understand.

1. A Positive Action Miracle:

This type of miracle adds a positive dimension to your life. Whether you get an unexpected raise or meet the man or woman of your dreams, these miracles increase the day-to-day quality of your physical life. The key to bringing positive action miracles into your life is to see all events as opportunities rather than obstacles. You should *desire* those opportunities, because they offer you an opportunity to transcend your nature. How? Obstacles trigger reactions within you. You worry. You fret. You stress. You whine. If you continue to do that, you can bet your bottom dollar that miracles aren't coming your way. If, however, you resist the desire to react to an obstacle, and you view it for what it really is—the chance to rise above your instinctive nature—a miracle of equal proportion is on the way to you. Make no mistake. This is how things really work.

2. A Removal Miracle:

This kind of miracle takes negative elements away from your life. Examples include being cured of a serious illness, having a difficult enemy suddenly move away to a new city (or better yet, to a new country!), or coming into unexpected money to remove all your debts and those nasty legal letters. These are all removal miracles.

The key to actualizing removal miracles is to see past the pain you feel right now. Whether it's physical, mental, financial, or spiritual in nature, whatever causes you pain also causes you to react to it. In this scenario, your reactions might include self-pity, feeling like a victim, or feeling sorry for yourself. This kind of "natural" behavior keeps natural laws of the universe in the status quo. When you accept responsibility for your pain, and realize it is payback from your own unkind behavior—in this life or a life past—you activate the power of miracles.

3. An Avoidance Miracle:

This is one of the most difficult miracles to recognize, because it involves knowing what *didn't* happen to you. Being delayed from arriving at the World Trade Center on September 11 would be a dramatic example, but many other such avoidance miracles happen all the time. Most of them go unseen.

Suppose you find out that a friend insulted you behind your back. You have good reason to blast that person. But having just finished a chapter of this *Miracles* book, you decide to resist the desire for vengeance. You rise above the emotions and pain, and you treat your friend with dignity and kindness. You realize that this was just the law of cause and effect playing itself out because you probably hurt this friend in another way at some earlier time.

Guess what? You now have a miracle coming your way, flowing from the 99% Realm.

A week later, you're driving to work. A car is destined to crash into you when you cross a particular intersection after the light turns green. The miracle energy surrounds you as you wait on a red light at that fateful intersection. All of sudden, you decide to change the radio station and search for better music. When you look down to scan the stations, you don't notice that the light has just turned green. A few seconds pass as you scan the radio. Suddenly, the car that was supposed to crash into yours passes through the intersection. Meanwhile, you find a great song on the radio. Now you look up, see the green light, and drive safely to work, never knowing how close you came to disaster.

4. An Incremental Miracle:

In some ways, this is the least dramatic type of miracle, but it's just as important as any of the others. Like most people, you probably work toward objectives that you really want to achieve in your life; this process can take years or even decades. Finding a spouse, building a home, having enough money to travel, or becoming a successful actor or singer are all examples. The incremental miracle occurs when something that *should* have taken a lot longer doesn't. One day, it just presents itself, in the form of love at first sight, an eager seller, a great business opportunity, or an unexpected phone call that propels you onto center stage. This isn't just "dumb luck" or "good fortune." You

made it happen each time you rose above
your ego and chose to proact instead of react!

You now know that you alone are responsible for producing all the miracles in your life, and this is the way
God intends it. As you gradually transform your nature,
step by step, you gradually unleash the power to perform miracles.

It happens measure by measure. Your degree of internal personal transformation corresponds directly to the
level of your miracle-making skill. If you're not attracting miracles, it's because you're the same person you
were 10, 20, or 50 years ago. However, the very act of
reading these pages is setting the process of change in
motion.

PAIN OR TRANSFORMATION

Your destiny is already set. Like all human beings, you're destined to possess the power of miracle making at will, having total control over the physical world, beyond what you can imagine at this moment. (Your ego will not allow you to accept this remarkable fact completely because that annoying curtain conceals such powerful truths). Nevertheless, you have two choices as to how you'll reach the state where you can produce miracles at will:

- You can get there through pain and suffering, which gradually erases the reactive egocentric character from your nature.

- You can proactively choose behavioral change and personal transformation, which simply means that you stop reacting to your ego. Actually, it's even simpler than that. Just stop reacting, *period*.

Clearly, the world has been evolving through the path of pain and suffering, but you don't have to remain on that course.

When you rise above your reactions and ascend above all the obstacles of this world, you are now in control of your life. You are now living under the influence of the 99% You instead of the 1% You. The moment you shut down the 1% You, the real you kicks in. The only pain involved is felt by your ego.

The ego hates to let go of its opinion. It always has to be right. It always has to be in control. It always has to talk and listen to its own voice.

Theory of Relativity

Make no mistake, ego is a relative concept; it's relative to each individual. For instance, one person's natural reaction may be to avoid the spotlight. The ego can make that person shy, timid, and unassuming. Such a person should go outside of himself and be more assertive, more passionate. If he wants to draw the power of a miracle, he should become the center of attention, no matter how frightening that prospect is.

On the other hand, another person's natural reaction may be to become the center of attention. She should steer clear of the spotlight, avoiding praise and attention like the plague if she wants to whip up a miracle.

The Process

Transformation can take an entire lifetime, or even two or three. But eventually the whole world will be free of its 1% Self and the power of the 99% Self will be in full bloom. Your goal of being the creator of your own miracles and happiness will be achieved.

The longer it takes you, the more painful the process. The quicker you change, the more pleasant and wondrous the path.

What follows next are some valuable techniques to speed your transformation and help you achieve the ultimate purpose of this book: to master the science of miracle making.

TECHNIQUE #1 GIVING: THE POWER OF TRUE CHARITY

There's an old saying: Give till it hurts. Before you got hold of this book, perhaps you didn't understand that saying. Now you do. If you give and it *doesn't* hurt, it's the 1% You who's doing all the giving.

1%ers love to give. They love to garner the respect, praise, and honor that accrues in the process. Tribute dinners, honorary awards, plaques, even hospital wings that bear the name of the donor are all trappings associated with charitable 1 Percenters. For all their generosity, these kinds of acts don't conjure up miracles. They merely redistribute material wealth and conjure up admiration and envy from colleagues, peers, and enemies.

According to *The Zohar*, true charity has the far greater power to remove judgment and death. It changes your life dramatically—but it has to hurt. A lot. It has to be transformative. You have to rise above your natural instinctive nature, which includes worry, doubt, and fear. When you do, the universe responds in equal measure.

Giving Anonymously

Kabbalah says that *concealed* charity is the most powerful form of giving. If other people know you give, you can be sure that the 1% You will derive enjoyment from the act, which undermines the power of any potential miracle. If the 1% You derives zero pleasure, the 99% You is now free to receive 100% of the benefit, and that means the ability to engineer the miracles you need.

When Fear and Doubt Are Good

Practicing true charity is one of the key factors in realizing miracles for yourself, but don't just take my word for it. Remember that vital kabbalistic principle: Try it out for yourself to see how true it is.

And remember, if you're not scared, fearful, and consumed with doubt a moment before you give, then you can't resist those emotions and attract a miracle after the giving is complete. So don't worry when doubts and fears attack you. That's your sign that the miracle is just waiting for you to make it happen.

TECHNIQUE #2
SEEK OUT THE UNCOMFORTABLE

If you're like most people, you love your comfort zone. You love being an armchair quarterback in the game of life, sitting back in your cozy, plush chair. But there's one problem with the comfort zone. Miracles never appear there. In fact, miracles are banned from the comfort zone. Miracles can only happen in the *Zone of the Terribly Uncomfortable*.

Situations that embarrass, scare, or humiliate you are fertile ground for producing miracles, both large and small.

Here's a true story of a small miracle that occurred when a good friend of mine practiced the art of miracle making by remaining in the *Zone of the Terribly Uncomfortable*. David Williams (not his real name) was in his mid-30s and extremely successful in business. The problem was, the 1% David had built the business. Thus, his ego was out of control.

I asked David to recount his story for this book.

Down and Out in Beverly Hills

When we came to California in 1994, I checked my family into the Beverly Hilton Hotel in Beverly Hills. It was, and still is, an expensive five-star hotel. I'd booked two rooms-one for my wife and myself, the other for my four kids and our nanny. We stayed at the hotel for about a month. Between restaurants, car rentals, and hotel costs, we ran up a bill of $50,000. I was making a lot of money, so I wasn't concerned. Actually, I was proud of the fact that I could afford it.

During our stay, the hotel concierge and staff got to know us and during our stay treated us really well, which made me feel very important. About a year later we returned to Los Angeles. When we pulled up to the hotel, the concierge recognized me and said, "Hello,

Mr. Williams. How are you? How are your kids?"

Wow! Now I really felt like a big shot. I thought I had arrived. Here I was at one of the most expensive hotels in Beverly Hills, and they still remembered me. They called me Mr. Williams! I was on cloud nine. Little did I know how worthless and pathetic those self-indulgent feelings were. But I quickly learned.

Eventually, my family and I moved to Los Angeles permanently. Within six months, I'd lost my entire business and all my money. We were broke. Seriously broke. When I say we had $20 in our pockets, it's not a metaphor. Thankfully, credit cards kept showing up in the mail and we lived on those for a year.

Meanwhile, we were forced to abandon our 10,000-square-foot home in Beverly Hills and move to a tiny duplex in West Los Angeles. I was shattered. Humiliated. Fortunately, I was becoming deeply involved in Kabbalah so I had tools and teachings to help me change my life.

One very hot summer day, my wife suggested we take our kids swimming. "Where?" I asked. My wife said we should sneak into the Beverly Hilton, pretend we were guests, and use their pool. Part of me enjoyed the adventure of sneaking in with my family, but another part was mortified by the thought. Only a short time ago I'd been "Mr. Williams," living like a king. Was I now reduced to parking my car a block away and sneaking in, pretending to be a guest? Knowing it would deflate my ego, I agreed to do it.

When we arrived at the hotel I was sweating bullets, but I held my head high as we walked through the front door and lobby in our bathing suits and went straight to the pool. The place was packed; we were lucky to find lounge chairs. As we walked through the pool area, I felt as if everyone was staring at me. I had this nagging feeling that they knew we were sneaking in. They could probably see it on my face. Then my worst nightmare came true.

The supervising pool attendant made a bee-line for us. She asked if we were guests of the hotel. I freaked. The sweat was pouring down my forehead-literally! I had a choice to make. Run out now with my family, looking like a bunch of idiots and fools and freeloaders in front of all the people at the pool, or answer her question and delay the inevitable-getting thrown out of the hotel in front of all these same people.

It would have been easier to not answer her and just walk out quickly. But I stayed. I

*answered her. I said, "Yes, we are guests."
She knew something wasn't right and she
asked to see my room key. "I don't have it
with me," I said. My kids thought I was nuts.
Now she knew something was up, and then
she delivered the hammer. "What room are
you staying in?" she asked. I had no time to
think. Not a second. I just blurted out a ran-
dom number: "Room 3325."*

*The first thought I had was, "OH NO! There's
probably NO such room!" It was such a crazy
number to blurt out.*

*Then she asked, "What's your last name?" I
said, "Williams." (I was too ashamed to say
"Mr. Williams.") She went over to the hotel
phone and made a call. I knew this was my
last chance to make a run for it, but I sum-
moned my Kabbalah wisdom and realized
that I should stay in the hot seat and soak up
the embarrassment. That's when I decided to*

accept my fate. And then I welcomed it. I was prepared and happy to be humiliated in front of all the affluent guests at the world-famous Beverly Hilton. My wife then said to me and the kids, "Don't worry. Everything will work out."

The pool attendant hung up the phone and walked over to us. She had a strange look on her face. She apologized profusely and said, "I'm so sorry Mr. Williams. Our records show that the Williams family checked out this morning. I guess that's why you don't have your room key." Then she brought us towels for the chairs, offered us a free room for the day, and bent over backward to make our afternoon as comfortable as possible.

Ten years later, I'm still shocked by this story. It was impossible; I don't know how it happened. It was a small miracle, but it showed me that if you're prepared to go the distance

*and climb out of your comfort zone, miracles
will occur and help you get out of even the
smallest jams in life.*

The lesson? By constantly stretching yourself and
escaping your comfort zone so that you transcend the
1% Self, you open the gates to miracles, large and small.

Here are a few helpful tips:

- Resist the desire to choose the fast and easy
  route. Hold steady to the challenging, obstacle-
  ridden path.

- Resist the desire to indulge your ego just so you
  can get rid of your insecurity. Instead, soak up
  the anxiety.

- Resist the desire to show off how smart or funny
  you are. Play that discomforting role of second
  banana. Or, if that's where you're most
  comfortable, step into the leadership role.

- Resist the urge to react with anger and show them who's boss. Let the other guy think he's better than you and enjoy the pain on your ego.

- Resist the desire to put others in their place when they wrong you, even if you're 100% right. Give them love and kindness instead.

Advice like this helps, but the truth is that you have to venture into the *Zone of the Terribly Uncomfortable* to witness and experience miracles for yourself. Then you'll come to know the power. You won't have to just take it on blind faith.

TECHNIQUE #3
ACTIVATE THE POWER OF
EXCITEMENT

A great kabbalist who lived some 500 years ago revealed an important secret and technique for activating the force called miracle. His name was Rav Isaac Luria, but he was known as *the Ari*, which means "the holy lion."

The Ari said that *excitement* is a key ingredient in the miracle-making formula. In other words, if you're depressed, doubtful, or cynical when seeking your miracle, that big old mirror in the sky will reflect depression, doubt, and cynicism back at you. That means no miracle.

If you're neck deep in a crisis, and you want to meditate, pray, and change your character to ignite a miracle, you must *also* arouse tremendous excitement and certainty at the same time. You must summon all the feelings you'd experience if the miracle was already right in front of your nose. You must behave *as if you already had the miracle*. You must ignite the same excitement, joy, and enthusiasm as if you were holding the miracle in your very hands.

Why? Follow this carefully.

If your certainty and excitement are *already* at the exact same level that they would be in the future, when the actual miracle does take place, then the mirror up there, that 99% Realm, must reflect that same excitement and certainty back to you *right now*. And the only way the 99% Realm can get you that excited and *that* certain is by *delivering you the actual miracle!*

Read technique #3 over a few times. This one takes a while to sink in.

TECHNIQUE #4
TAKE RESPONSIBILITY FOR
EVERYTHING

What's the origin of all chaos and pain in your life?

Your reactive behavior toward others.

There it is, like it or not. It's not the people you dislike. It's not that you're overweight, unattractive, or not bright enough. It's not your diet. It's not corrupt politicians. It's not acts of God such as earthquakes, floods, and deadly viruses. And it's not the family that you're born into. In fact, the ancient *Zohar* reveals a startling truth—children actually choose their parents before the moment of conception occurs. A child's soul selects the appropriate family in which to be born.

There goes that excuse! You chose your parents. Your children chose you. You all chose one another because all the souls knew ahead of time which baggage everyone would be bringing to the table. That baggage serves one single great purpose—to trigger reactions within you, because that gives you the opportunity to rise above those reactions and create miracles.

Yes, life is just that simple. The problem is that 99.999% of the time, you react. You respond. You lash back. You allow everyone to push your buttons all day long. So, nothing changes. Miracles don't happen. And you blame the world.

Who Cares about Morals!

If you need a miracle of any kind, you must take responsibility. You must become accountable for your misfortune. Not because you believe it's the right thing to do. Rubbish! Kabbalah doesn't care about morals and ideals. Kabbalah is about the self-interest of the soul. When you take responsibility, you ignite the power of miracles. *You* benefit from that action.

What's In It for Me?

If you couldn't score a miracle through responsible behavior and proactive living, you'd never find the motivation to become accountable and proactive. Morals don't provide you with enough motivation. On paper, maybe. Intellectually, for sure. But in real life, never. Morals have never changed anyone, and they never will.

When you finally wake up and realize that *you* are the cause of your own chaos and you genuinely accept that harsh truth 100%, you'll rise above the 1% Self and make contact with the 99% Realm, the source of all miracles.

That's the payoff for taking responsibility! You become a miracle producer in the process.

THE REALLY TOUGH MIRACLES

Becoming accountable for whatever ails you is easy to describe but very difficult to achieve. Never, ever underestimate the challenge of accepting all the blame for your misfortune. Especially when a serious illness strikes, or a severe financial problem hits. It's so easy to be told what you need to do to solve a problem, but it can be nearly impossible to practice it when you find yourself in the grip of a crisis.

So, sit down for a moment. Quiet your mind. Open your heart. Let go of all your doubts, *just for a moment*. Let go of all your preconceived notions about life and death, healing and medicine, and all the social conditioning and pop-cultural influences that have impacted your life.

Be still.

Now read this carefully . . .

Heart Attacks

Suppose a person is diagnosed with high cholesterol and the doctor discovers serious blockages in his arteries. A cardiologist usually prescribes various cholesterol-lowering drugs to treat the symptoms.

Did you know that medical science was only able to identify cholesterol, fatty deposits, and blocked arteries as the major cause of heart attacks as recently as the 1980s?

The year was 1984. A report published by the U.S. National Institutes of Health entitled "Lowering Blood Cholesterol to Prevent Heart Disease" stated the following:

- Cholesterol is a fatty substance. There are two kinds:

- "Bad" cholesterol, which tends to clog blood vessels; and

- "Good" cholesterol, which actually helps unclog the arteries.

Too much bad cholesterol can block your arteries and cause heart attacks, strokes, and death. Not nice.

Good cholesterol removes bad cholesterol and thus helps prevent heart attacks. Nice. Fats work the same way. There are good fats, which unblock arteries, and bad fats, which clog them.

Now here comes a mindblower

According to *The Zohar*, your reactive 1% emotions—notably anger, rage, ego, and envy—all manifest in your liver. This is the underlying cause of heart disease, illness, and death. As *The Zohar* puts it:

> *"From the liver . . . emerges the bile, which is the sword of the Angel of Death. From the bile come bitter drops to kill human beings."*

The Zohar goes on to say that the bitter drops that come from the liver and bile "are offered to the heart" if you are reactive. These bitter drops then "overcome the arteries of the heart and all the arteries in the limbs of the body."

Now guess what?

Cholesterol comes from the liver. The liver secretes bile, and bile's primary component is—you guessed it—cholesterol!

The Zohar also says that if you're proactive, behaving with kindness, then your liver produces "pure fatty substances" that are offered to the heart through the arteries, which bring you health.

Both the ancient Zohar and modern-day science agree: Blockages in your arteries from bad cholesterol cause heart attacks, strokes, and death. Good cholesterol and good fats help prevent such diseases.

THE CAUSE OF CAUSES

So, what's the origin of all disease? *Your behavior toward others*, either from this life or from past lives. You can deny it. You can laugh about it. Or you can accept it and start changing your world.

Health is not about the foods you eat. In the end, it's not really about your DNA or your genes. Those are merely the weapons used to inflict negative karmic payback upon you—payback that has its origins in your own actions of ego and intolerance. Who pulls the trigger to activate disease and allow these foods or genes to kill you? You do.

In other words, *The Zohar* asks: Why does a soul choose a body with a specific DNA and a predisposition to disease in the first place? Why does a soul choose to be born into a particular family in this physical world? And why do some genes that cause disease get activated while others remain dormant? Why does one person in a family who smokes one pack of cigarettes a day get a heart attack, but another person in that same family who smokes five packs a day live to see 100?

Here's *The Zohar*'s answer

An unknown assailant shoots someone in a dark alley, killing him instantly. The final police report, which costs the taxpayers a bundle, describes precisely how the bullet did its damage, smashing through this bone and that tissue.

Pretty useless information, right? Why? Because the next week, the murderer strikes again, shooting and killing someone else. This time we get another police report, which costs taxpayers another fortune and explains how this bullet wrought its unique brand of havoc on the victim. But Kabbalah asks, who cares about the physics of bullets striking human flesh and bone?

The gun is only a weapon. The bullet is merely another weapon.

Instead, we want to know:

Who pulled the trigger?

Once the police catch the murderer, then we will have arrived at the root cause of the killings. All those endless medical studies that you read about each day in the newspaper concerning the causes of heart disease and every other illness miss the point entirely! To find the real cause, you must look much closer to home.

BUSINESSES HAVE HEART ATTACKS, TOO

The Zohar explains that blockages in the arteries can also occur in other areas of life. Ultimately, all the ills of society have one root cause—people's interactions with one another.

Essentially, all relationships in life are "arteries." Relationships are the key to everything! For instance, a blockage can occur in a marriage relationship. When this particular artery is blocked, love and passion can no longer flow between a husband and wife. Call it a heart attack, or a death in a marriage.

Your various business relationships are also arteries, only they connect employers and employees, wholesalers and retailers, sellers and buyers.

The money that flows to you through the deals you make or the work you do travels through these arteries. When they're clogged by greed and ego, then good fortune fails to flow to you. Keep in mind that if you cheat in business, these blockages might also wind up in the physical arteries of your body. In other words, you might prosper in business despite underhanded dealings, but you might pay for it with a triple bypass or rotten relationships with your children.

All the relationships of the world—between people, between business partners, between brother and sister, between husband and wife, between parents and children, between one nation and another—are spiritual arteries that can become blocked and cause disease when people behave with intolerance toward one another.

Each time you interact with someone in your life— friend or stranger, enemy or family member—you affect the arteries in your life that extend out into the world. If your behavior in those relationships is governed by the 1% You and self-interest, it creates a "fatty deposit." If the blockages continue to grow unchecked, "disease" sets in.

This disease can manifest itself as poverty, war, divorce, kids on drugs, anxiety, a dysfunctional family, global terrorism, or a good old-fashioned heart attack. In the end, your behavior determines good health or poor health.

ROOTING OUT THE CULPRIT

It's so easy to blame diet, fate, nature, crooked business partners, genes, drunk drivers, or your enemies for your pain and suffering.

It's too darn easy to focus upon the weapon and not the true culprit.

This kind of approach to life absolves you from all personal responsibility. And after all, who wants to look in the mirror? Which leads to a most important question:

How do you conjure up a miracle that will cure you of disease, be it in business, marriage, or health?

As we've discussed, the first step is accountability. And this is, without question, the most difficult step of all to take.

You must lose the victim mind-set. You must realize that it was something you did, in this life or a past life, that caused the sickness. Next, you must focus upon transforming the specific trait responsible, the negative quality in your character that caused you to behave reactively at some earlier point.

This accomplishes two things:

1. Taking responsibility is totally out of character for a human being. Thus, you've just shut down your 1% Self and made an internal change within. That's a miracle, and the universe must reflect that miraculous effort back into your life.

2. By searching out the actual trait that caused you to react in the first place, and exerting the effort to remove it from your nature, you've just made another internal change in your character. Once again, the 99% Realm will mirror this miraculous change and send you a miracle in return.

When you accept responsibility—100%—then and only then can the tools of Kabbalah arouse the Light of the Creator so you can be healed.

THE MIRACLE-MAKING TECHNOLOGY

The methodology is simple, but the practice is not. Making miracles is challenging, no doubt about it. Because it is such a challenge, the ancient kabbalists offered the tools we've discussed to help you accelerate the process of unleashing your true self, the 99% You.

This book was written to share with you the technology of miracle making while giving you an understanding of how reality works and why it works the way it does. In other words,

- **You now know the nature of reality.** A curtain divides reality into two: the 99% Realm, the source of all miracles and joy; and the 1% Realm, the source of all chaos and pain.

- **You now know why you're here.** We humans asked the Creator to hide all the happiness and miracle-making power behind the curtain so we could create our own happiness and miracles through our own effort right here in the 1% Realm.

- **You now have the formula for manufacturing miracles.** You must resist the impulses of your ego and your 1% nature. The degree of your miraculous change of nature in a given situation conjures up an equal measure of miracle energy from the 99% Realm. The more you change, the greater the number of miracles you'll receive. The more significant your change, the more significant your miracles will be. Because miracles are extraordinary events, you must perform extraordinary positive actions to attract such supernatural forces.

Letting go of anger, revenge, worry, fear and accepting blame for all the rotten stuff that happens to you in life is a monumental task. It's a huge undertaking. By no means underestimate the power of the 1% You. It has many layers and veils, which take a lifetime to remove. However, each time a veil is removed, each time you conquer the 1% You, you receive a miracle in return.

If you choose to embrace Kabbalah's path of transformation, your entire journey will be filled with wonders and miracles, large and small, all along the way. That's better than a path of pain. The good news is that you can speed up the process of attracting greater and more wondrous miracles. Oh, you'd like to know how? Okay. This is where we can discuss the use of additional tools.

Technology for the Soul
Kabbalah is all about technology, not religion (which requires taking things on faith). There are a number of books that contain more technology needed to connect you to the 99% Realm. I recommend the following: *The Zohar; The 72 Names of God,* and *The Red String Book.*

Once you've established a connection to the 99% Realm, you draw energy into your life. This energy gradually tears away the veils of the 1% You. The more you use the technology, the more strength and power you acquire to rise above your reactions.

So, now you have it. Are you excited? Are you full of passion?

These secrets, though written here in a simple and lighthearted fashion, are thousands of years old and deeply powerful. A lot of blood was spilled over the centuries, trying to keep this wisdom from people like you and me. By the way, your appreciation of this fact will actually assist you in drawing miracles to your life.

MAKE A MIRACLE NOW

Here's your first chance to truly bring about a small change in your character right now. Appreciate the wisdom in this book. Deeply. Stretch yourself. Go deep inside and find a way to be thankful and grateful for the opportunity to learn a bit about life, according to the wisdom of Kabbalah. Keep in mind, the kabbalists of history would never request your appreciation. You aren't doing it for them. You're doing it for yourself. True appreciation takes a small measure of character change, and that's how you manufacture miracles.

When you feel true appreciation for this wisdom, you'll get a miracle in return.

When you get your miracle, feel free to write me a letter, email me, or log on to 72.com and share your story. And remember,

"There is no problem a good miracle can't solve."
—Unknown

As part of an ongoing commitment to bring you technology that transforms lives, we're developing a coaching program over the phone. Soon, you will be able to work one-on-one with a dedicated Kabbalah coach who will help you develop your ability to create miracles in your own life on a regular basis.

If you were inspired by this book in any way and would like to know how you can continue to enrich your life through the power of Kabbalah, here is what you can do next: Read the book *The Power of Kabbalah* or listen to the *Power of Kabbalah* audio tapes.

The Power of Kabbalah

Imagine your life filled with unending joy, purpose, and contentment. Imagine your days infused with pure insight and energy. This is *The Power of Kabbalah*. It is the path from the momentary pleasure that most of us settle for, to the lasting fulfillment that is yours to claim. Your deepest desires are waiting to be realized. But they are not limited to the temporary rush from closing a business deal, the short-term high from drugs, or a passionate sexual relationship that lasts only a few short months.

Wouldn't you like to experience a lasting sense of whole-ness and peace that is unshakable, no matter what may be happening around you? Complete fulfillment is the promise of Kabbalah. Within these pages, you will learn how to look at and navigate through life in a whole new way. You will understand your purpose and how to receive the abundant gifts waiting for you. By making a critical transformation from a reactive to a proactive being, you will increase your creative energy, get control of your life, and enjoy new spiritual levels of existence. Kabbalah's ancient teaching is rooted in the perfect union of the phys-ical and spiritual laws already at work in your life. Get ready to experience this exciting realm of awareness, meaning, and joy.

The wonder and wisdom of Kabbalah has influenced the world's leading spiritual, philosophical, religious, and sci-entific minds. Until today, however, it was hidden away in ancient texts, available only to scholars who knew where to look. Now after many centuries, *The Power of Kabbalah* resides right here in this one remarkable book. Here, at long last is the complete and simple path—actions you can take right now to create the life you desire and deserve.

The Power of Kabbalah Audio Tapes

The Power of Kabbalah is nothing less than a user's guide to the universe. Move beyond where you are right now to where you truly want to be—emotionally, spiritually, creatively. This exciting tape series brings you the ancient, authentic teaching of Kabbalah in a powerful, practical audio format.

You can order these products from our Web site or by calling Student Support.

Student Support: Trained instructors are available 18 hours a day. These dedicated people are willing to answer any and all questions about Kabbalah and help guide you along in your effort to learn more. Just call **1-800-kabbalah**.

MORE PRODUCTS THAT CAN HELP YOU BRING THE WISDOM OF KABBALAH INTO YOUR LIFE

The Red String Book: The Power of Protection
By Yehuda Berg

Read the book that everyone is *wearing!*

Discover the ancient technology that empowers and fuels the hugely popular Red String, the most widely recognized tool of kabbalistic wisdom. Yehuda Berg, author of the international best-seller *The 72 Names of God: Technology for the Soul*, continues to reveal the secrets of the world's oldest and most powerful wisdom with his new book, *The Red String Book: The Power of Protection*. Discover the antidote to the negative effects of the dreaded "Evil Eye" in this second book of the *Technology for the Soul series*.

Find out the real power behind the Red String and why millions of people won't leave home without it.

It's all here. Everything you wanted to know about the Red String but were afraid to ask!

The Dreams Book: Finding Your Way in the Dark
By Yehuda Berg

In *The Dreams Book*, the debut installment of the Technology for the Soul Series, national best-selling author Yehuda Berg lifts the curtain of reality to reveal secrets of dream interpretation that have remained hidden for centuries.

Readers will discover a millennia-old system for understanding dreams and will learn powerful techniques to help them find soul mates, discover career opportunities, be alerted to potential illness in the body, improve relationships with others, develop an overall deeper awareness, and much more.

The dream state is a mysterious and fascinating realm in which the rules of reality do not apply. This book is the key to navigating the dreamscape, where the answers to all of life's questions await.

God Wears Lipstick
By Karen Berg

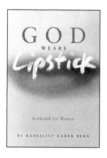

For 4,000 Years, Kabbalah was forbidden to women—until one woman decided that was long enough.

In directing Kabbalah Centres worldwide with her husband, Rav Berg, Karen Berg opened the world's most ancient form of wisdom to everyone on earth—for the first time.

Now, in *God Wears Lipstick*, she reveals women's special spiritual role in the universe.

Based on the secrets of Kabbalah, *God Wears Lipstick* explains the spiritual advantage of women, the power of soulmates, and the true purpose of life, and conducts a no-holds-barred discussion of everything from managing relationships to reincarnation to the sacred power and meaning of sex.

The 72 Names of God: Technology for the Soul™
By Yehuda Berg

The story of Moses and the Red Sea is well known to almost everyone; it's even been an Academy Award–winning film. What is not known, according to the internationally prominent author Yehuda Berg, is that a state-of-the-art technology is encoded and concealed within that biblical story. This technology is called the 72 Names of God, and it is the key—your key—to ridding yourself of depression, stress, creative stagnation, anger, illness, and other physical and emotional problems. In fact, the 72 Names of God is the oldest, most powerful tool known to mankind—far more powerful than any 21st century high-tech know-how when it comes to eliminating the garbage in your life so that you can wake up and enjoy life each day. Indeed, the 72 Names of God is the ultimate pill for anything and everything that ails you because it strikes at the DNA level of your soul.

The power of the 72 Names of God operates strictly on a soul level, not a physical one. It's about spirituality, not religiosity. Rather than being limited by the differences that divide people, the wisdom of the Names transcends humanity's age-old quarrels and belief systems to deal with the one common bond that unifies all people and nations: the human soul.

Becoming Like God
By Michael Berg

At the age of 16, Kabbalistic scholar Michael Berg began the herculean task of translating *The Zohar*, Kabbalah's chief text, from its original Aramaic into its first complete English translation. *The Zohar*, which consists of 23 volumes, is considered a compendium of virtually all information pertaining to the universe, and its wisdom is only beginning to be verified today.

During the ten years he worked on *The Zohar*, Michael Berg discovered the long-lost secret for which mankind has searched for more than 5,000 years: how to achieve our ultimate destiny. *Becoming Like God* reveals the transformative method by which people can actually break free of what is called "ego nature" to achieve total joy and lasting life.

Berg puts forth the revolutionary idea that for the first time in history, an opportunity is being made available to humankind: an opportunity to Become Like God.

The Secret
By Michael Berg

Like a jewel that has been painstakingly cut and polished, *The Secret* reveals life's essence in its most concise and powerful form. Michael Berg begins by showing you how our everyday understanding of our purpose in the world is literally backwards. Whenever there is pain in our lives—indeed, whenever there is anything less than complete joy and fulfillment—this basic misunderstanding is the reason.

The Essential Zohar
By Rav Berg

The Zohar has traditionally been known as the world's most esoteric and profound spiritual document, but Kabbalist Rav Berg, this generation's greatest living Kabbalist, has dedicated his life to making this wisdom universally available. The vast wisdom and Light of *The Zohar* came into being as a gift to all humanity, and *The Essential Zohar* at last explains this gift to the world.

Power of You
By Rav Berg

For the past 5,000 years, neither science nor psychology has been able to solve the fundamental problem of chaos in people's lives.

Now, one man is providing the answer. He is Kabbalist Rav Berg.

Beneath the pain and chaos that disrupts our lives, Kabbalist Rav Berg brings to light a hidden realm of order, purpose, and unity. Revealed is a universe in which mind becomes master over matter—a world in which God, human thought, and the entire cosmos are mysteriously interconnected.

Join this generation's premier kabbalist on a mind-bending journey along the cutting edge of reality. Peer into the vast reservoir of spiritual wisdom that is Kabbalah, where the secrets of creation, life, and death have remained hidden for thousands of years.

Wheels of a Soul
By Rav Berg

In *Wheels of a Soul*, Kabbalist Rav Berg reveals the keys to answering these and many more questions that lie at the heart of our existence as human beings. Specifically, Rav Berg explains why we must acknowledge and explore the lives we have already lived in order to understand the life we are living today . . .

Make no mistake: *you have been here before.* Reincarnation is a fact—and just as science is now beginning to recognize that time and space may be nothing but illusions, Rav Berg shows why death itself is the greatest illusion of all.

In this book you learn much more than the answers to these questions. You will understand your true purpose in the world and discover tools to identify your life's soul mate. Read *Wheels of a Soul* and let one of the greatest kabbalistic masters of our time change your life forever.

THE KABBALAH CENTRE
The International Leader in the Education of Kabbalah

Since its founding, The Kabbalah Centre has had a single mission: to improve and transform people's lives by bringing the power and wisdom of Kabbalah to all who wish to partake of it.

Through the lifelong efforts of kabbalists Rav and Karen Berg, and the great spiritual lineage of which they are a part, an astonishing 3.5 million people around the world have already been touched by the powerful teachings of Kabbalah. And each year, the numbers are growing!

May all who see the letters below
Awaken in their heart and soul
The ancient wisdom therein unlock:
We alone create our own miracles.

Kuf Nun Mem

With blessings, love, and Light to our Creator.

Donna